Queen Bee Mathematical
and the Number Garden Friends

Pandora Alexander Walker

AuthorHouse™
1663 Liberty Drive
Bloomington, IN 47403
www.authorhouse.com
Phone: 833-262-8899

Because of the dynamic nature of the Internet, any web addresses or links contained in this book may have changed since publication and may no longer be valid. The views expressed in this work are solely those of the author and do not necessarily reflect the views of the publisher, and the publisher hereby disclaims any responsibility for them.

This book is printed on acid-free paper.

ISBN: 978-1-6655-3484-0 (sc)
ISBN: 978-1-6655-3485-7 (e)

Print information available on the last page.

Published by AuthorHouse 08/16/2021

authorHOUSE®

ACKNOWLEDGMENTS

I would like to thank my husband, my editors, my children, and my family, without whose help this book would never have been completed. Thank you for your patience and time.

DEDICATION

I dedicate this children's books to my children, Michael Keith Fontenett and Mariah Ann Fontenett, and my grandchildren, Kayson Michael Fontenett and Kylan Keith Fontenett.

Meet Queen Bee Mathematical. Beem is her play name.

Beem lived in a land close to everyone. She had a garden of numbers that was her pride and joy. She loved counting, adding, subtracting, multiplying, and dividing the numbers.

Her workers buzzed around the numbers and flowers. The sunshine and rain helped them to grow.

While the number garden slept, beetles crept from stem to stem, and night creatures crawled within. There was a change coming to the number garden. That night, the wind blew fiercely and brought with it some strange birds.

Morning came, and Beem was awakened by one of the strange birds flying about her window and tapping on it. So, out of curiosity, she opened the window and noticed more birds—blue, yellow, gray, and red—dropping the letters "x" and "y" into the number garden. Bee Mathematical wanted to take a closer look at her garden and the letters left there.

Beem could hear the birds singing The Mystery Letters Song as they left the letters "x" and "y," replacing some of the numbers.

"Balance one thing with the others and soon you will undo the letters."

Bee Mathematical would need all her royal subjects and friends to help undo the letters in her number garden left by the strange birds.

She was puzzled by the x's and y's.

Beem called her royal subjects. Pi was the first because he was somewhat of a mystery number. He would often change from a floating decimal to a fraction.

After Pi, she called Imaginary, or "I," as most everyone in the kingdom referred to him.

Imaginary knew how to find numbers in both real and imaginary places in the kingdom.

Bee Mathematical's workers memorized the Mystery Letters Song and hummed it while they worked to unravel the mystery. With all her subjects busy working together and searching near and far, Beem would undo the letters "x" and "y" in her garden.

They all kept thinking about the song: "Balance one thing with the others and soon you will undo the letters."

Pi and Imaginary realized that the letters were placeholders just like them, so the letters "x" and "y" must have number values.

They asked Beem to get them a scale so they could check the letters and numbers in the garden.

Pi and Imaginary used the first clue: "Balance one thing with the others."

They took the numbers and letters and began weighing them on the scale.

After trial and error, they realized which one balanced the other.

They weighed the numbers and letters until the scale was even. "The mystery is solved!" they all sighed out loud.

"Balance one thing with the others and soon you will undo the letters."

Queen Beem and her subjects now live happily with the numbers and letters in the garden. They are happy they solved the mystery in the number garden.

They continued to sing the number and letter song: "Balance one thing with the others and soon you will undo the letters."

THE END

About the Author

Mrs. Walker has a Master of Education in Educational Leadership for grades EC–12, a Bachelor of Science degree in Mathematics, several certificates in mathematics for AP Mathematics, and Gifted and Talented certifications from College Board. She has worked for several school districts in Texas, where she served as district lead teacher, curriculum writer, lead teacher, and department chair. When Mrs. Walker started tutoring students, she found no books that show math in a positive light, so she wrote this book and several others to help parents both entertain their kids and teach them about math.

Other Stories in the Bee Mathematical Series include:

Pie Who I am I?

The Summation of All Things

The Number Friends, LOL!

Glossary

Numbers are mathematical values used for counting and measuring objects, and for performing arithmetic calculations. Numbers have various categories like natural numbers, whole numbers, rational and irrational numbers, and so on.

Natural numbers are all positive **numbers** like 1, 2, 3, 4, and so on. They are the **numbers** you usually count, and they continue till infinity.

Example: Natural Numbers or Counting Numbers but **without the zero 1, 2, 3, 4, 5, ...**

Whole numbers are all-natural **numbers** including 0, for example, 0, 1, 2, 3, 4, and so on. Integers include all whole **numbers** and their negative counterpart.

Example: Whole Numbers and natural numbers that include "0" 0, 1, 2, 3, 4, 5, ... (and so on)

Rational Number are numbers that can be written as a Ratio (fraction) of two integers.

Example: 1.5 is rational, because it can be written as the ratio 3/2

Irrational Numbers some numbers cannot be written as a ratio of two integers ...

Example: π (Pi) is a famous irrational number. π = 3.141592653 5897932384626433832795... (and more) We cannot write down a simple fraction that equals Pi. The popular approximation of 22/7 = 3.1428571428571... is close but not accurate.

Real Numbers are all the above whole, rational and irrational numbers.

Example: Whole Numbers (like 0, 1, 2, 3, ...) Rational Numbers (like 3/4, 0.125, 0.333..., 1.1,)

and Irrational Numbers (like π, Euler's "e", √2, ...) Real Numbers can also be positive, negative or zero.

Integers are like whole numbers, but they also include *negative* numbers!

number line -10 to 10 So, integers can be negative {−1, −2, −3, −4, ...}, positive {1, 2, 3, 4, ...}, or zero {0} We can put that all together like this:

Example: Integers = {..., −4, −3, −2, −1, 0, 1, 2, 3, 4, ...}

Imaginary numbers are numbers that is expressed in terms of the square root of a negative number (usually the square root of −1, represented by i).

Examples:
$$\sqrt{-9} = \sqrt{9 \times -1} = \sqrt{9} \times \sqrt{-1} = \pm 3i$$
$$\sqrt{-4} = \sqrt{4 \times -1} = \sqrt{4} \times \sqrt{-1} = \pm 2i$$

Balancing Scale in mathematics we use this tool to strengthen understanding and computation of numerical expressions and equality. In understanding equality, one of the first things students must realize is that equality is a relationship, not an operation.

Example:

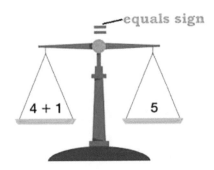

Variable is a symbol for a value we don't know yet. It is usually a letter like x or y. In mathematics formulas have will have variables or a placeholder for an unknown quantity. Pi is often used as placeholder for the approximated value 3.14.

Example: unknown value "x" makes the statement true x +2 =6

Area of a circle A= πr^2 where radius is 6 or A =(3.14) (6^2)

Printed in the United States
by Baker & Taylor Publisher Services